Proceeds from the sale of this book benefit organizations dedicated to promoting spiritual growth, world peace and global healing.

PEACEFUL EARTH

PEACEFUL EARTH:

Spiritual Perspectives
on Hope and Healing
Beyond Terrorism

Compiled by
Lisa Hepner

Hold
the
Vision

Hold the Vision
www.peacefulearth.org

Peaceful Earth: Spiritual Perspectives on Hope and Healing Beyond Terrorism.

Hold the Vision/December 2001

CATALOGING-IN-PUBLICATION DATA

Peaceful Earth : spiritual perspectives on hope and healing beyond terrorism / compiled by Lisa Hepner. –1st ed.
   p. cm.
   ISBN 0-9715845-9-1

   1. September 11 Terrorist Attacks, 2001 --Religious aspects--Christianity. 2. Terrorism--Religious aspects --Christianity. 3. Peace--Religious aspects-- Christianity. 4. Spiritual life--Christianity.
   I. Hepner, Lisa Ann.

   BT736.15.P43 2001   261.8' 73
                        QBI01-201378

PRINTED IN THE UNITED STATES OF AMERICA
PRINTED USING RECYCLED PAPER

This book is dedicated to all those searching for greater wisdom and Truth regarding the recent tragedy in America.

May you find love, comfort, peace and healing from the insights in this book.

"Returning violence for violence only multiplies violence, adding deeper darkness to a night already devoid of stars.
Darkness cannot drive out darkness; only light can do that. Hate cannot drive out hate; only love can do that."

Dr. Martin Luther King, Jr.

TABLE OF CONTENTS

Let There Be Peace On Earth

Let there be Peace on Earth,
and let it begin with me.

Let there be Peace on Earth,
the Peace that was meant to be.

With God as our Father, brothers all are we.
Let me walk with my brother, in perfect harmony.

Let Peace begin with me,
let this be the moment now.

With every step I take,
let this be my solemn vow—

To take each moment and live each moment,
in Peace eternally,

Let there be Peace on Earth,
and let it begin with me.

By Sy Miller

A Prayer for World Peace

I know there is but One Mind, which is the mind of God, in which all people live and move and have their being.

I know there is a divine pattern for humanity and within this pattern there is infinite harmony and peace, cooperation, unity, and mutual helpfulness.

I know that the mind of humankind, being one with the mind of God, shall discover the method, the way, and the means best fitted to permit the flow of divine love between individuals and nations.

Thus harmony, peace, cooperation, unity, and mutual helpfulness will be experienced by all.

I know there shall be a free interchange of ideas, of cultures, of spiritual concepts, of ethics, of educational systems, and of scientific discoveries—for all good belongs to all alike.

I know that, because Divine Mind has created us all, we are bound together in one infinite and perfect unity.

In bringing about world peace, I know that all people and all nations will remain individual but unified for the common purpose of promoting peace, happiness, harmony, and prosperity.

I know that deep within every person the divine pattern of perfect peace is already implanted.

I now declare that in each person and in leaders of thought everywhere this divine pattern moves into action and form, to the end that all nations and all people shall live together in peace, harmony, and prosperity forever.

And so it is now.

By Ernest Holmes

Introduction

The pain and grief from the recent terrorist attacks cannot be denied. It has touched all of our lives in one way or another. We are inundated with messages from the media of retaliation and attack, and we are bombarded with images of the horrific footage of planes crashing into the World Trade Center.

Everyone is searching for ways to deal with this tragedy. Everyone is filled with unanswered questions and uncertainty. How do we cope? Where do we go from here? What is the "right" response? What role does prayer have in any of this? These are questions posed by everyone from all walks of life.

The purpose of this book is to address all the questions surrounding the terrorist attacks from a spiritual reference point, or a higher consciousness. The media has expressed their views and the government has referenced their strategies. But many of us want to know "What would love do here?" What is the "highest good?" and "How can we help, collectively, to make the world a better place in order to prevent future atrocities?"

Now it's time to take a look at the recent tragedy from a spiritual perspective from some of the greatest spiritual leaders of our time.

September 11, 2001 will be a date recorded in history. Let this book be a spiritual message of peace, love and healing that will also go down in history as a compilation of thoughts from a higher perspective of Truth, insight and wisdom.

May the following words and insights provide support and comfort and invoke a healing inside of you, and may you take that experience with you to help others heal, and to help heal the planet. May we all experience love, peace and healing.

While you are proclaiming peace with your lips,
be careful to have it even more fully in your heart.

St. Francis of Assisi

Peace

Vrede

Salaam

He Ping

Mir

Paix

Hetep

Frieden

Sipala

Religious Fanaticism

September 11, 2001: A Day to be Remembered!

I'm sitting watching Bryant Gumble on CBS. I'm in Lake Charles, Ontario, Canada. It's about 8:30 am.

Bryant ends the segment saying, "When we return, we have some breaking news concerning an accident...a fire...at the World Trade Center."

"I wonder what's happened now?" I muse. I continue to drink my coffee.

Bryant continues, "when we return the World Trade Center is on fire. A plane has crashed into the building."

"How sad," I think. "Poor pilot must have had a heart attack and lost control and hit the building. I do hope they put the fire out soon."

Then the unspeakable happens. The unexpected. The inexplicable happens. Another plane, a commercial jet hits the other tower. Calamity. Catastrophe. War.

The coffee is allowed to go cold. Words, mere words, which are my tools of trade, cannot explain what has just happened. In a matter of moments the world has changed forever.

I switch to CNN, CNBC. Every station in Canada is carrying the burning of the World Trade Center.

I pinch myself. Am I dreaming? Is this a movie? Remember when Orson Welles told Americans that creatures from Mars were invading? Is this some sick joke?

A news break. An airplane has crashed into the Pentagon. The Pentagon is on fire. Where is the President? Is he safe?

America is at war. The unthinkable is now being discussed on TV in the way we discussed the tax cut. Same anchors. Same voices. Different world.

I have a lecture to give at 9:30 am. I switch off the TV and walk towards the lecture hall. Two hundred people are waiting for me. They eat doughnuts, drink coffee, and discuss last night's ball game. They are all unaware of the news.

"Father Leo, you're late."

"A disaster has hit America. The World Trade Center is on fire...the Pentagon has been hit...I can't believe what I've been watching. New York is covered in smoke."

"Are your books for sale? Do you have hand outs?"

How can they understand? They didn't see it. I saw it and I still don't understand!

The workshop continues. I'm a professional. But I don't really know what I'm saying. I'm on remote.

People enter the workshop looking worried. Others leave and return. Soon everybody is looking concerned, worried, and confused.

The workshop ends. Televisions are brought into the luncheon. Nobody really speaks. Few eat.

"Father Leo, will you pray with us?"

"Sure."

What do I say? Words seem inadequate. They don't really want words. A gesture. A sound. A cry for help...to God.

People come over to thank me. Many are crying. They remember previous wars. Trauma. Fear. Faith.

September 11, 2001; an ordinary day that in minutes, became extraordinary.

War...in God's name.

"What is the Holy Jihad, Father Leo? Have we gone back to the days of the Crusades? Christians killing Muslims? Or in this case, Muslims killing Christians?"

"Well, Bob, it's important to remember that it is <u>some</u> Muslims, not all. Most Muslims want peace. They've lived alongside people of other faiths for years with no problem. But there are fanatics. Fanatics are like another religion, a non-love, non-compassion, and non-logical kind of religion that thinks only in terms of black and white. No compromise and no gray areas. And the fanatic is always right!"

Most Muslims want peace. They've lived alongside people of other faiths for years with no problem. But there are fanatics. Fanatics are like another religion, a non-love, non-compassion, and non-logical kind of religion that thinks only in terms of black and white. No compromise and no gray areas. And the fanatic is always right!"

Bob is my neighbor. He occasionally comes over and has a sandwich with Hilary, my housekeeper. He loves sandwiches. Naturally, he has a great friendship with Hilary!

"Jihad is a holy war?"

"That's what I understand, Bob. Christians don't use that word, but many Christians over the years have felt it was right and proper to go to war against obvious evil. Hitler and the Second World War is a good example.

It is true that some Christians are against <u>all</u> wars, but I would say that most Christians felt it was 'correct' to go to war against Hitler. Now, although as I'd said we don't use the word 'jihad' you could say that we were applying the concept of jihad for a greater good; a righteous war!"

"Is that what Osama bin Laden is conducting?"

"That is what he says he is conducting against America. I'm sure he would also include Great Britain. He says America is evil. Maybe he truly thinks that. He excuses his behavior and the actions of his followers in this way.

"Personally, Bob, I believe he is a terrorist. A religious, fanatic terrorist. Consumed by his own anger towards America, Great Britain, and the Western world and as a result he has become evil, corrupt and detestable."

"How can this happen to a human being?"

Bob is a good man who spends most of his time gardening. Occasionally, he visits his grand-children, and often calls my home for a sandwich. Terrorism, religious fanatics, and obsessive behavior are not part of his world.

"I wrote a book about these issues called, *When God Becomes a Drug: Understanding Religious Addiction and Abuse.* I appeared on Oprah and talked about crazy religion. The book became popular, but you know, Bob, most people didn't really believe that crazy religion could be dangerous."

"Well, they're finding out now."

Bob was shaking his head as he walked home muttering, "They're finding out now."

- Crazy people make for crazy religion.
- Unhealthy people often have unhealthy beliefs.
- Fanatics are always dangerous; religious fanatics doubly so. They speak in God's name.
- In the wrong hands, the Bible or the Koran can be a dangerous book.

This outrage that was perpetrated on September 11th has its roots, not just in political terrorism, but in its subtle and little discussed relative:
religious (addiction) fanaticism.

This outrage that was perpetrated on September 11th has its roots, not just in political terrorism, but in its subtle and little discussed relative: religious (addiction) fanaticism.

Father Leo Booth

Peace

Shalom

Pace

Pax

Taika

Shanti

Nirudho

Sula

Paz

Faith Keeper

In the Native American tradition, one member of the tribe assumes the role of "Faith keeper." This person's role is to remain at peace, centered in spiritual vision, no matter what events befall the tribe. Even if everyone else in the tribe slips into pain, fear, or dissension, the Faith keeper is the one person the tribe can rely on as a lifeline to the Presence. This is our role now.

In the face of the strange and shocking events that have recently occurred, it would be almost humanly impossible not to be moved and to feel challenged. Who could look upon such inhumanity and not be shaken?

Yet there is a place within all of us that is always connected to our higher being. That is the place to go to now. Your greatest contribution is your clarity, sense of purpose, and vision. If you go into fear or terror, the terrorists have won. They have succeeded in terrorizing you. Is that the role you would play? Would you not rather overcome hatred with love? Doubt with trust? Sorrow with comfort?

Your greatest contribution is your clarity, sense of purpose, and vision. If you go into fear or terror, the terrorists have won.

"Fear knocked at the door. Faith answered. No one was there."

The question is not, "Have you moved off your center?" The question is, "How quickly can you regain it?"

For many years we have been studying the principles of spiritual truth. Now is the time to put them into practice. When things are going well, it is easy to find God. When things seem chaotic, it is harder.

The strength we build by claiming divine order when it is utterly unapparent is paramount. Spiritual mastery is gained in times such as these.

As you may know, I find many practical spiritual lessons through stories in motion pictures. One comes to mind now that is quite applicable: In "Starman," an extraterrestrial visits earth to experience the joys and sorrows of life as a human. He develops a relationship with a woman who loves him. Eventually he must return to his home planet, but before he does, she asks him what he has learned about the people of earth.

"When things are at their worst," he comments, "you are at your best."

September 11th showed us a disaster unlike any that most of us have seen in our lifetime. But September 12th and the days that follow have shown us an outpouring of love and compassion unlike any we have seen in our lifetime.

No single event has connected so many people throughout the entire planet with a sense of caring and support. People from all over the world are reaching out to share resources, blood, skill, money, and heart. There is a miracle in here somewhere.

No single event has connected so many people throughout the entire planet with a sense of caring and support

---

Let us not use this event as a way to stay disconnected from higher power. Hold firm to your sense of wholeness and to the wholeness of everyone you consider. When you are upset, you are ineffective to see a right course of action. When you are hooked up, you are very powerful.

Mahatma Gandhi noted, "The pure love of one person can offset the hatred of thousands." The pure love of one person can offset the anxiety of thousands. Let us each be that one person.

Mahatma Gandhi noted, "The pure love of one person can offset the hatred of thousands."

There are two elements to this event: What happened, and what we do with it. What was done has been done. What will be is still in our hands. We can make of it what we choose. We can use it as a justification to lash out or we can build a new consciousness that has no home for terror.

Let us stop terrifying ourselves with scary thoughts. Love disarms.

We bless and send love and intentions for

well being to those most affected. Words soothe little, but respect for your power edifies you.

When one of my parents passed away, a friend left a simple message on my answering machine that helped me immensely: "I feel your strength."

We stand in deep honor of the leaders and people of New York, who are demonstrating immense courage and cooperation. New Yorkers are compellingly resilient, and they will prevail.

Thank you for an awesome model of dignity and grace under fire. Perhaps it is no accident that world attention is being focused on the World Trade Center.

Perhaps the message is that it is time to trade our old world for one more connected to our center.

Perhaps the message is that it is time to trade our old world for one more connected to our center. We will come out on the other side of this. We will pick up the pieces and move on. And we will be closer to home for it.

Alan Cohen

The War Within

In times of challenge it is most important to be courageous, positive, and enthusiastic. I know that this is the most difficult thing to do, as it is a natural tendency to fall into a heap of sorrow, hopelessness, and fear.

We have two egos: our true spiritual self and our worldly self. Our work is to recognize our true spiritual self and to bring forth and express this self of love, bliss, beauty, strength, and intelligence rather than to allow fear, doubt, and negativity to take control and destroy us.

Let us look at what has happened from a metaphysical standpoint. Each of us has terrorized ourselves at some point. This happens when the false self that is steeped in fear, greed, envy, and poverty has taken over.

We must do battle with this lower Self and endeavor to have our higher Self win out or we are lost and defeated by our own minds. The outer world is an out picturing of our inner world; therefore our work is to create our inner world, as we desire it to be.

The outer world is an out picturing of our inner world; therefore our work is to create our inner world, as we desire it to be.

The lesson is to never allow fear, hate, anger, negativity, or miserliness to control us, but to rise above these mental terrorists by learning and applying the principles of successful living.

It is our inner world that manifests in the outer. In each moment we are given the opportunity to choose love or hate, peace or fear, faith or doubt, happiness or misery, etc.

It is a time for spiritually minded people to take a stand for what is good, holy, loving, and divine by choosing to honor the Godlike self in every situation and encounter.

It is a time for spiritually minded people to take a stand for what is good, holy, loving, and divine by choosing to honor the Godlike self in every situation and encounter.

Fear is a horrible feeling and it causes people to do horrible things. Envy is the disease of human kind and the cure is knowing that God loves us all, whatever the religion, nationality, color, sex, or culture.

There is more than enough for all of us to live together in peace and plenty. The worst thing that anyone can do during these times is to lose faith in God and revert to fear, doubt, weakness, and depression.

Spiritual people must be courageous and be willing to take a stand for what they know to be true, by living it at all times.

Now, more than ever, we need to think positive, do good, inspire and uplift others, take spiritual classes, read spiritual books, attend and serve in our place of worship, see the good in others, work to bring forth our true self as we defeat the false, and make a difference in the lives of others, as best we can.

We are praying for those who have gone on and we must also pray and act for peace in the world.

The best way to bring peace in the world is to be peaceful. The best way to create love is to give love.

The best way to bring peace in the world is to be peaceful.

The best way to manifest a good life is to control your mind and keep it elevated, and in each encounter choose to honor that which is for the highest of all concerned.

What I am doing during this time is traveling throughout the United States and the world and teaching the principles of Successful living.

This is my way of uplifting human kind. Think of what you can do to make your own life magnificent and to reach out to others and uplift them.

One person helping another is the way we will learn to love, and whatever the problem, love is the solution. Knowledge will liberate us from fear, war, poverty, and ignorance.

Instead of fearing, the best thing we can do is use sacred knowledge to build our inner world and outer world, as we desire.

No matter what happens in this world the laws of the Universe and the spiritual principles remain the same and are applicable to all alike. The laws that govern the universe, and our lives, do not change. It is we who must change our consciousness and behavior.

As Winston Churchill said, "The only thing we have to fear is fear itself."

Let us win the war that is within us, the one that is going on in our own minds. Most people are tormented by fear, doubt, poverty, misery, anger, greed, envy, and jealousy.

When God is our mutual Source and Supply we only see love. Now it is time to prove our faith and to act from our true self in every situation.

Let us win the war that is within us, the one that is going on in our own minds.

This is our test of faith, and we shall be victorious.

Dr. Terry Cole-Whittaker

God is Good

Grace is when you take nothing and turn it into something; or when you are able to take tragedy and pain and create a positive experience out of it. It says in the Old Testament, "Without vision, the people perish." My question to each and every one of you is, "What is your vision?" Is it one of peace? And can we take the tragedy of September 11th and turn it into a positive scenario?

"Without vision, the people perish."

The Peace Song says, "Let there be peace on earth and let it begin with me." The key words being "begin with ME." Because that's where peace happens. Peace happens within, then manifests in the outer world.

Many of you may wonder what good can come out of September 11th? The story that comes to my mind is the story of Joseph and his many-colored coat. Joseph was the most illuminated of all his brothers. Because of this his brothers conspired against him and did mean, awful and terrible things to him and left him for dead.

Joseph ends up in a prison in Egypt and interprets the dreams of the guard keeper. The prison guard takes him to the Pharaoh who had been having a recurrent dream he couldn't quite understand.

Joseph tells the Pharaoh that he is going to have seven years of feast and seven years of famine. Joseph tells the Pharaoh that he will get to control the whole world if he is wise and prudent and listens to him and saves twenty percent of everything.

Israel starts starving. Joseph's father sends all the brothers to Egypt to see if they can bring back food to Israel. The brothers have no idea that it's their little brother who they will have to negotiate with. The brothers cower before Joseph. You can imagine how they felt after wishing him nothing but harm and now needing to ask him for food.

Joseph says to them, "what you meant for my harm, God meant for my good." (Genesis 50:20.)

Joseph says to them, "what you meant for my harm, God meant for my good."
                                        Genesis 50:20.

What Bin Laden meant for our harm, God meant for our good.

I am invited to spcak at the President's dinner honoring the heroes of September 11th. The hero I am honoring is the pilot who understood that terrorism was going on, because the World Trade Center had already been slammed into, and pulled the fuel so that the plane would go down in the middle of nowhere thereby not harming any more people. Now, that's an American hero. This type of heroism is being witnessed everywhere.

Since September 11th, we have better communication, more prayer, and more people attending church now than ever before. We're finally starting to understand who we are in God and who God is, in us.

We're finally starting to understand who we are in God and who God is, in us.

Are we going to let terrorism prevail? NO.

I put together a CD with a phenomenal speaker and entrepreneur, Debra Jones. It's about beating terrorism. It's called "Let's Keep America going." For more information you can go to the website at www.letskeepamericagoing.com.

But basically it says that, if you can shop and you don't shop, then the economy drops and terrorism wins. If you can tithe and you don't tithe, terrorism wins. If you can volunteer and you don't volunteer then terrorism wins.

Terrorism wins by immobilizing us, by keeping us scared, by making us think about how small we are instead of acknowledging our big Self.

John Denver said, we drink the same water, and we breathe the same air and we have to make the planet work for 100% of us. We are all one. Don't think about how scared you are to fly now, think about how by flying, you will be creating a strong economy. We must take individual action to make a collective difference.

We've got to keep giving. What makes America great is our capacity to give. Many people think, "if only I had more, I'd give more." Or, "if I had it, I'd give it." Yet most people don't realize that the reason we got it, is because we keep giving it.

What makes America great is our capacity to give.

The more you give, the more you get. We must remember that God is the Universal source and that there's more than enough for everyone. And finally, the Kingdom of Heaven is inside, not outside. Therefore, peace resides within, before it manifests outwardly.

Mark Victor Hansen

Global Union

We are all New Yorkers!!!

That is the gist of the message that I have been receiving from the thousands of e-mails, countless phone calls and faxes, and communications from people writing or calling me from over thirty countries.

The outpouring of love, of service, and even of life itself is the miracle of humanity surpassing itself. All over this country and throughout the world people are affirming their unity with us, and more, the unity of all people.

This tragedy brings us together in shadow and in light, for richer and for poor, in sickness and in health for as long as we all shall live.

The desecration that has occurred is also the announcement of a potential global union.

I have often spoken of how technology and the Internet gave us the "world mind" taking a walk with itself. But in the light of the events of September 11th, we now must speak of the "world heart," the "world stomach," and the "world spirit."

America is no longer insulated from the pathos of other nations. We are present at the birth of an opportunity that exceeds our imagination.

We are present at the birth of an opportunity that exceeds our imagination.

Christopher Fry wrote, "Thank God, our time is now, when wrong comes up to meet us everywhere, never to leave us till we take the longest stride of soul men ever took."

All oppression rises in our time, all shadows, all terrors, and all factors unique in human history also arise around us to compound our folly and confuse our desire.

We yearn for meaning and deal with trivia. We are swept in currents over which we have no control.

Government has become too big for the small problems of life and too small in spirit for the large problems.

Government has become too big for the small problems of life and too small in spirit for the large problems.

The tyranny that threatens to destroy us is not just terrorism; it is the tyranny of the unjust demands we have made of Nature and the tyranny of some nations being kept in economic slavery by other nations.

We are the ones who have the most profound task in human history—the task of deciding whether we grow or die. This will involve helping cultures and organizations to move from dominance by one economic culture or group to circular "invested ness," sharing and partnership.

It will involve putting economics back as a satellite to the soul of culture rather than having the soul of culture as satellite to economics.

It will involve deep listening past the arias and the habits of cruelty or crushed and humiliated people. It will involve a stride of soul that will challenge the very canons of our human condition. It will require that we become evolutionary partners with each other.

This is a huge test we find ourselves in. We have newly emerged from a century of war and holocaust. Our hopes for the new century and the new millennium, was for a new way of being between nations and people, between the earth and us, between spirit and matter.

Those hopes still live, if anything, they have become more powerful and more necessary. For America, it will mean a deep shift of our attitudes from exploitation and dominance of other cultures around the world to service and support of them.

Yes, the perpetrators have to be found and dealt with through therapeutic law and International justice.

They are not a nation, they are a cancer, and a cancer is rarely removed through a cycle of violence. Rather, as in holistic Medicine, they have to be subdued by the strengthening of the healthy immune system, the envisioning of the pattern of health, and yes, the removal of the cancer wherever it can be excised.

The metaphor is apt. Our health, our security, is built on friendship. Instead of spending billions of dollars on weapons of destruction (which we manufacture ourselves and sell globally), what if we were to use some of that money to feed the hungry (one in every three persons), house the homeless, and make efforts to heal the wounds of nations. Real security demands real friendship, or Global marriage.

One of my correspondents who brilliantly addressed these issues said, "The problem is not just terrorism. The problem is generations of beings who experience not having an identity. The question is, what made human beings incapable of feeling love, compassion or empathy towards themselves or anyone else, and thereby, becoming destroyers of their own species?

What happened that human beings could become so psychologically, emotionally and spiritually distorted that they could believe that Islam, one of the most spiritual paths in the world, could encourage murder and suicide to gain heavenly reward?"

Friends, these are not Muslims. These are marginalized fanatics who have made a travesty of their faith. The issue is how we can join together to create a world in which such pathology will no longer be nurtured.

The issue is how we can join together to create a world in which such pathology will no longer be nurtured.

Many of us are feeling impotent before the enormity of the prospect. Some of you, I know, have experienced "meltdown", some have seen visions, had dreams. Many have had the portals of their minds blown open to deeper realities, potent reflections.

Tragedy has drawn us closer, sent us deeper, and given us the option of preparing for life rather than death.

I have been considering some of the things that you may wish to do in the days and weeks to come that will give expression to your feelings and need to act.

What I offer below is drawn primarily from my own reflections as well as others, particularly some prescriptions offered by Yes! Magazine. (www.yesmagazine.org)

1. In these spirit quaking times, align with your own spiritual resources. Take time to meditate, pray, reflect in solitude and in nature. Allow yourself daily time and space to be re-sourced. Consider living daily life as a spiritual exercise. Watch your finer intuitions and ideas, and share them with others. Commune with your spiritual allies, archetypal friends, and quantum partners. In the place of spiritual connection, feel strength and compassion and intelligence flow. Become creative in your actions. Plot scenarios of optimal healing and begin, wherever you can, to put them in place for events, as well as people. Practice miracle management.

2. Give yourself vacations from television. Most of it is filled with Infomercials for war, anyway. (However the local New York City

stations are filled with human stories of compassion and courage.)   Listen occasionally to talk shows and call in with your own opinions and ideas for making a better world. For inspiration and wisdom to deal with the challenges of our time, listen to New Dimensions Radio on your public radio station or on the Internet, (newdimensions.org).

3. Write a letter to the editor. Write or call your congressman and local government officials. Handwritten faxes seem to be the things that are most likely to get through, followed by phone calls. E-mails alas are the least likely. You can find your U.S. representatives at www.house.gov and your Senators at, www.senate.gov. Above all, let your voice be heard!

4. Gather in groups and, if possible, in ongoing teaching-learning communities of wisdom and empowerment. But let everyone speak, and do not deny them the authenticity of their feelings, even if they diverge widely from your own.

5. Talk to kids, your own or other people's children. Let them express their feelings, and tell you what is on their minds. Give them a grasp of the larger issues at hand. Tell them about mercy and compassionate action. If possible engage them in service-oriented activities. Let them see the larger story.

6. Show up at town meetings, or other places where people meet to pray and talk and engage each other. Sign petitions, if you are willing, and join in other activities that are "sending a big message". Create vision circles to put forth images of what the world can be. Envision the possible society together. (For ideas, you might want to look at my book, authored with Margaret Rubin, *Manual of the Peacemaker*, which deals with the Iroquois creation of a better society.)

7. Get thee to a mosque! Give support and compassion to Arab friends, colleagues, or people you happen to meet of Middle Eastern origin. Stamp out hatred and fear surrounding these people wherever you can. Let them tell their stories, their hopes and dreams. In fact, try and learn as much as you can about the Middle East, the political situations there, as well as the teachings of Islam. For key information on the crisis and well-considered information and opinions about the Middle East you may want to go to Alternet.org and commondreams.org.

8. Give up your own holding patterns on your old self. This is the time to become, or at least to enact, the possible human. Let your senses take pleasure in the glory of this world. Let your heart celebrate the incredible gift of life. And share this with others.

I live in a double domed house that was the last design of my old friend Buckminster Fuller, completed just before he died. I asked my house what words it would give you and it responded with Bucky's own. They came out of a time of tremendous personal crisis in his life.

"So I vowed to keep myself alive, but only if I would never use me again for just me - each one of us is born of two, and we really belong to each other. I vowed to do my own thinking, instead of trying to accommodate everyone else's opinions, credos and theories. I vowed to apply my own inventory of experiences to the solving of problems that affect everyone aboard planet Earth."

"...I vowed to do my own thinking, instead of trying to accommodate everyone else's opinions, credos and theories. I vowed to apply my own inventory of experiences to the solving of problems that affect everyone aboard planet Earth."

Jean Houston

Cooperation

When a catastrophic event occurs, powerful feelings may arise. If this tragedy had been a tornado or earthquake, it would have represented a destructive blip in nature's enigmatic scheme. But this was personal; human beings did this deliberately to other human beings.

These events remind us that while we cannot control circumstances in the world or in our personal lives, or guarantee our personal safety, we can choose how we will respond to whatever happens.

So I offer this: Let's not give more power to a small group of zealots; let's not let them live in our heads rent-free. Let's not react as they wish — to bring the entire country to a halt and create waves of paralysis farther-reaching than the localized damage they caused.

Let's not give more power to a small group of zealots; let's not let them live in our heads rent-free.

We cannot and should not try to stop or control our natural emotional reactions, but we can thwart their nefarious goals by responding, within our immediate circle of friends, with compassion and calm.

Once their damage is done, terrorists can only haunt our lives with our cooperation; let's not give it to them. Let's reclaim our power over our own psyches, behavior, and lives.

---

*Once their damage is done, terrorists can only
haunt our lives with our cooperation;
let's not give it to them.*

Our country has been called a sleeping
giant, and the world knows it's resolve when
roused. Justice will prevail. But what form that
"justice" may take is difficult to predict. We can
pray (and contact our representatives) that our
government acts with wisdom. We are not likely
to think without acting, but neither should we act
without thinking.

We cannot fix the world with good intentions alone. But we can remember to breathe
deeply, to relax our bodies, to focus on the present
moment, and to do what needs to be done in the
coming days and weeks.

Lawns still need mowing; children and pets
need care. Against the backdrop of the news and
larger world; we have our smaller world, and we
have this moment.

Life has elements of uncertainty, but one
thing I know: Every adversity has the potential
to bring new lessons and growth. We have seen
the outpouring of heroism and sacrifice, of love
in many forms, and have experienced a newfound
sense of unity as Americans —Muslim, Christian,
Jewish, Buddhist, Hindu Americans— all of us in
this together.

*Every adversity has the potential to bring
new lessons and growth.*

You and I can go on with our lives —
sobered, matured, with a new perspective and
new appreciation for what we have. This is the
end of our childhood.

Let's pray for those who need it and turn
our prayers into kind actions; let's accept our
emotions without letting them disable our clarity;
let's keep our hearts open, even to the waves
of fear, sorrow, and anger that arise naturally,
like passing storms; and let's resolve to do what
we can, in our own humble ways, to help create
a world of understanding, compassion, courage,
and love — beginning with ourselves.

Dan Millman

Peace

Mire

Fois

Hau

Sidi

Su Thai Binh

Sholem

Sulh

Nei

Peace after Terrorism

September 11th was a day that changed all our lives.

First came, shock, horror, and disbelief, as we watched America under attack. Later, in the midst of our mourning, stories of tremendous heroism, courage and love emerged, and it is those stories that provide us a template for our own lives.

...stories of tremendous heroism, courage and love emerged, and it is those stories that provide us a template for our own lives.

We may feel scared at times—uncertain about the future— we may feel insecure about our finances in an ever-changing economy. We may fear for our own safety. These feelings can lead to a sense of helplessness. We cannot control events that spring from a mind of hatred.

But we are not at all helpless. We can find a way to live in peace regardless of circumstances. I was struck by the cell phone calls the victims made from the World Trade Center, from the airplanes about to crash. Notice there wasn't one person saying, "I want to make a quick sale in the stock market." They were saying, "I want to talk to my loved one. I want to call the people I love and tell them one last time how much I love

them." Because when it really comes down to it;
that's what matters.

Love is eternal, profound and real. The love
we have for one another and the relationships we
develop, matter when nothing else does.

I saw an interview in which a man talked
about the last conversation he had with his wife,
who was aboard one of the doomed flights. She
told her husband how much she loved him and
that she truly believed that although her plane
had been hijacked, everything would be fine. But
it was not. That night, he could not go to bed.
Of all things, that day had been his birthday.
Finally, when he did go to bed, he found on his
pillow a note from his wife proclaiming her love
for him and how much he mattered to her.
What a simple act. She wrote a note. What a
treasured, treasured gift that note has become
now.

So I must wonder how often we don't recognize how important our expressions of love are.
We think of love as a feeling. But it is also an
active verb. We need to think about how often we
say, "I love you" to those who matter. We need to
think about how often we praise and acknowledge
the people in our lives. We need to consider the
acts of kindness we perform, not only for our
loved ones, but also for everyone in our path.

---

*So I must wonder how often we don't
recognize how important our expressions of
love are.*

That love is something nobody can take from us. The more we love one another, the stronger we become as individuals, and the stronger we become as a nation.

We have an opportunity now for a resurrection as we have never known it before; a resurrection of all that is good and true and holy— the very foundation of our country, a country that is formed out of the opportunity of liberty and freedom and differences.

Love doesn't stop at our doorstep. We can embrace those who think and believe and worship differently than we do without diminishing ourselves.

Love doesn't stop at our doorstep. We can embrace those who think and believe and worship differently than we do without diminishing ourselves.

I'm reminded of what Abraham Lincoln said: "Let us re-adopt the Declaration of Independence and with it, the practices and policy, which harmonize with it. Let North and South, let all Americans, and let all lovers of liberty everywhere join in the great and good work. If we do this, we shall not only save the Union, but we will have so saved it that the succeeding millions of free, happy people, generation after generation, the world over, shall rise up and call us blessed to the last generation."

    Let us rise to the occasion. The future of our country, of our very planet, depends on us moving from Guidance, as a global family. There is no force greater than the power of love.

There is no force greater than the power of love.

Mary Manin Morrissey

A Transformative Paradigm:

The Key to An Enhanced Human Life

New Thought philosophy teaches us that we are a life form of God and, as such, we are activities of this divine creative energy, which is the essence of our true self. As activities of God, we are always expressing the wonders of creation through our innovations, new concepts and new ideas.

The key to an enhanced life is the expanded awareness of this truth of our being. Unfortunately, the vast majority of the world population is not aware of this truth of being.

Many people do not reach this level of awareness and, rather than identifying themselves with God, the source of all supply, they identify themselves with the outer experience.

As a result of being in this lower state of awareness, should a perceived tragedy occur, whether it be a shortage in cash flow, a relationship which is on the edge, a health problem, or a problem at work, or a terrorist attack, they focus on the problem and become part of it, and in the process, destroy their well being.

As a result of being in this lower state of awareness, should a perceived tragedy occur, they focus on the problem and become part of it, and in the process, destroy their well-being.

William James, the great Psychologist told the world in the late eighteen hundreds that most people live, whether physically, intellectually or morally, in a very restricted circle of their potential.

William James said that, "People make use of a very small portion of their possible consciousness, much like the man who, out of his whole body organism, should get into the habit of using and moving only his little finger."

The change of awareness from identification with the external human condition to an identification with our inner creative source of all good takes us out of the box of this restricted circle of potential and opens us up to the unlimited creative force of the Universe, the dimension of infinite possibilities.

This is the meaning of transformation, a movement in consciousness resulting in a change in the awareness of the nature of our being. This requires a commitment to our own education. Many people view education as a place or an institution. Education is not a place confined to four walls, it is a state of consciousness that exists in the NOW wherein the individual is available to what life is presenting in the moment.

This understanding of education implies that it is a lifelong learning process. Each day brings us new experiences and new challenges that ultimately bring us closer to God. Therefore, each day of our life is a learning experience, and our growth comes from being open and receptive to the new and not contaminating the

NOW with the identification of the past.

Each day brings us new experiences and new challenges that ultimately bring us closer to God.

Making ourselves available to what life has to offer means that we discard old worn out beliefs and concepts that do not serve us any longer. We expand our understanding by attending conferences and retreats, taking classes, and surrounding ourselves with people of like minds.

We look at life as a wonderful gym with many opportunities to practice and we look forward to what life has to offer, knowing that every moment brings us, through a learning process, closer to the awareness of the source of all good, the key to an enhanced human life.

Through this process of life long learning, we gradually become fully aware that we are magnificent activities of God and we begin to grow spiritually into self-actualization, where our potential becomes our reality. Our potential is our ability to live the nature of God, every moment of the day. This means that love prevails in the face of anger and hatred, and that abundance prevails in the face of poverty.

---

*This means that love prevails in the face of
anger and hatred, and that abundance prevails in
the face of poverty.*

We are activities of God and when we
come to full awareness and realization of this, we
transform our lives and experience the awesome
reality that "it is all good and it is all God."
And So It Is!!!!

Dr. Angelo Pizelo

Why did God let this happen?

On a number of occasions I have been asked what my spiritual perspective is on the recent events of September 11th. I would first like to offer my deepest sympathy to the many individuals who lost loved ones. And, although nothing I have to say will ease the heartache of those who are suffering, we do know— time will lighten the load.

I believe it is worth remembering that both science and theology clearly indicate that nothing is created or destroyed, which leads us to postulate the theory that there is only life, there is no such thing as death. We do not have a soul; we are a soul. We moved into our body and we will most certainly move out of it. Our lost loved ones are still with us in spirit and we will join them— we just do not know how soon.

I believe this was best expressed by Theodore Roosevelt who wrote the epitaph for his son who was killed in action; six months before his own death. He wrote, "Only those are fit to live who do not fear to die and none are fit to die who have shrunk from the joy of life. Both life and death are parts of the same great adventure."

All of those who provide service and stand ready to sacrifice are the torchbearers. "We run with the torches until we fall, content if we can pass them to the hands of the other runners."

There are many individuals who are plagued with the question, "Why did God let this happen?"

God had nothing to do with it. God gave

every human being the power to choose and never interferes with our choices.

There are many individuals who are plagued with the question, "Why did God let this happen?" God had nothing to do with it. God gave every human being the power to choose and never interferes with our choices.

To help us understand this better we might ask why did God let some young punk snatch the purse out of the hand of an elderly lady? Or, why did God let some brute of a man rape and terrorize an innocent woman? Or, why did God permit one person to murder another? God had nothing to do with any of these acts of violence.

The only difference between any of them or any other act of violence and what happened on September 11th is our perspective. I am certain if it was my daughter or wife who was brutalized and raped or murdered, the tragedy to me and the impact on my life would be every bit as great as it would be to anyone who lost a loved one in those towers.

There are many things in life that we do not understand and this tragedy very likely falls into that category with most people; certainly it does with me. However, regardless of what happens, I believe in God and I believe that God is the creator, the architect of the universe. I also believe that God operates in a very precise way that is often referred to "by law." The spirit of

God never expresses itself other than perfectly. The imperfection is in our individual or collective ways of thinking and acting.

The spirit of God never expresses itself other than perfectly. The imperfection is in our individual or collective ways of thinking and acting.

Everywhere you look in nature, you will see the hand of God at work. Nature is perfect and surrounds us as a model to emulate. Our objective in life should be to gain an understanding of God's laws and attempt to bring every facet of our lives into harmony with those laws. It is my opinion that we are here to do God's work. God, being the creator, God's work is creation. Unlike any other form of life, we were given creative faculties— one of those creative faculties is our ability to reason and it is with reason that we are able to choose. And, as I've already stated, God never interferes with our choices.

The heroes, who gave their lives on September 11th, as well as all of the occupants of those buildings, were torchbearers. All were providing service and the police and fireman were certainly standing ready to sacrifice and, in fact, made the ultimate sacrifice with their lives. In truth, they were doing God's work; they were creating.

I have come to realize that one of the laws

of the universe is the law of polarity or the law of opposites. It clearly indicates that everything has an opposite, there would be no inside without outside, an up without down or hot without cold. The opposite of bad is good. If something is only a little bad, when you mentally work your way around to the other side of it, you will find just a little good. If something is fairly bad, it's polar opposite is fairly good.

The tragedy of September 11th was huge. The good that can and will come from it is equally as huge. However, we will only benefit from the good that can come from this tragedy by looking for it, as difficult as that might be, and then utilizing it.

The tragedy of September 11th was huge. The good that can and will come from it is equally as huge.

Out of all confusion comes order, a higher degree of order than that which existed prior to the confusion. The negative impact of this event can be so deeply imbedded in our subjective mind that it has the potential to dominate our thinking. We must not permit that to happen. We must consciously and deliberately work at developing the higher faculties we were blessed with and use them to search for, find and apply the good that can come from such enormous loss.

We must consciously and deliberately work at developing the higher faculties we were blessed with and use them to search for, find and apply the good that can come from such enormous loss.

This, of course, is not easily done and it will not happen by accident. Nor will it happen by letting ourselves be wired to the negative broadcasts that dominate our media. We must recognize the acts of courage that are taking place in New York every day and the good that is being done by people worldwide and directed towards those who are suffering. Good and bad, creation and destruction are choices. We must make certain that we do not permit the perpetrators of this tragedy to cause us to follow their path, by focusing on the negative.

Good and bad, creation and destruction are choices. We must make certain that we do not permit the perpetrators of this tragedy to cause us to follow their path, by focusing on the negative.

Let's rejoice in the fact that all those souls who are gone are with God, they have made the transition and moved on to the next phase of their eternal journey. We can look forward to that day, full of wonder, when we will join them. And we must never forget that God is good— all the time.

Bob Proctor

Peace

Ukuthula

Dohiyi

Mir

Mutenden

Pake

Sulh

Fred

Fois

We Are One

The events of September 11, 2001 cause every thinking person to stop their daily lives, whatever is going on in them, and to ponder deeply the larger questions of life. We search again for not only the meaning of life, but the purpose of our individual and collective experience as we have created it—and we look earnestly for ways in which we might recreate ourselves anew as a human species, so that we will never treat each other this way again.

The hour has come for us to demonstrate at the highest level our most extraordinary thought about Who We Really Are. There are two possible responses to what has occurred. The first comes from love, the second from fear.

There are two possible responses to what has occurred. The first comes from love, the second from fear.

If we come from fear we may panic and do things—as individuals and as nations—that could only cause further damage. If we come from love we will find refuge and strength, even as we provide it to others.

A central teaching of Conversations with God is: What you wish to experience, provide for another.

What you wish to experience, provide for another.

Look to see, now, what it is you wish to experience—in your own life, and in the world. Then see if there is another for whom you may be the source of that.

If you wish to experience peace, provide peace for another.

If you wish to know that you are safe, cause another to know that they are safe.

If you wish to better understand seemingly incomprehensible things, help another to better understand.

If you wish to heal your own sadness or anger, seek to heal the sadness or anger of another.

If you wish to heal your own sadness or anger, seek to heal the sadness or anger of another.

Those others are waiting for you now. They are looking to you for guidance, for help, for courage, for strength, for understanding, and for assurance at this hour. Most of all, they are looking to you for love.

This is the moment of your ministry. This is

the time of teaching. What you teach at this time, through your every word and action right now, will remain as indelible lessons in the hearts and minds of those whose lives you touch, both now, and for years to come.

We will set the course for tomorrow, today. At this hour, and in this moment. There is much we can do, but there is one thing we cannot do.

We cannot continue to co-create our lives together on this planet as we have in the past. We cannot, except at our peril, ignore the events of this day, or their implications.

It is tempting at times like this to give in to rage. Anger is fear announced, and rage is anger that is repressed, and then, when it is released, it is often misdirected. Right now, anger is not inappropriate. It is, in fact, natural—and can be a blessing.

If we use our anger about the recent events not to pinpoint where the blame falls, but where the cause lies, we can lead the way to healing.

Let us seek not to pinpoint blame, but to pinpoint cause. Unless we take this time to look at the cause of our experience, we will never remove ourselves from the experiences it creates. Instead, we will forever live in fear of retribution from those within the human family who feel aggrieved, and, likewise, seek retribution from them.

Let us seek not to pinpoint blame, but to pinpoint cause.

So at this time it is important for us to
direct our anger toward the cause of our present
experience. And that is not necessarily individuals or groups who have attacked others, but,
rather, the reasons they have done so. Unless
we look at these reasons, we will never be able to
eliminate these attacks.

To me, the reasons are clear. We have not
learned the most basic human lessons. We have
not remembered the most basic human truths.
We have not understood the most basic spiritual
wisdom. In short, we have not been listening
to God, and because we have not, we watch
ourselves do ungodly things.

The message of *Conversations with God* is
clear: we are all one.

We are all one.

That is a message the human race has
largely ignored. Our separation mentality has
underscored all of our human creations. Our
religions, our political structures, our economic
systems, our educational institutions, and our
whole approach to life have been based on the
idea that we are separate from each other. This
has caused us to inflict all manner of injury, one
upon the other. And this injury causes other
injury, for like begets like and negativity only
breeds negativity.

It is as easy to understand as that. And

so now let us pray that all of us, in this human family, will find the courage and the strength to turn inward and to ask a simple, soaring question: what would love do now?

What would love do now?

If we could love even those who have attacked us, and seek to understand why they have done so, what then would be our response?

Yet if we meet negativity with negativity, rage with rage, attack with attack, what then will be the outcome?

These are the questions that are placed before the human race today. They are questions that we have failed to answer for thousands of years. Failure to answer them now could eliminate the need to answer them at all.

We should make no mistake about this. The human race has the power to annihilate itself. We can end life, as we know it, on this planet in one afternoon.

The human race has the power to annihilate itself.

This is the first time in human history that we have been able to say this. And so now we must direct our attention to the questions that such power places before us.

And we must answer these questions from a spiritual perspective, not a political perspective, and not an economic perspective.

We must have our own conversation with God, for only the grandest wisdom and the grandest truth can address the greatest problems that we are now facing and the greatest challenges in the history of our species.

It is not as if we have not seen this coming. Every spiritual, political, and philosophical writer of the past fifty years has predicted it. So long as we continue to treat each other as we have done on this planet, the circumstance that we face on this day will continue to present itself.

The difference is that now our technology makes our anger much more dangerous. In the early days of our civilization, we were able to inflict hurt upon each other using sticks and rocks and primitive weapons. Then, as our technology grew, it became possible for clans to war against clans and, ultimately, for nations to war against nations. But even then, until most recent times, it was not possible for us to annihilate each other completely.

The difference is that now our technology makes our anger much more dangerous.

We could destroy a village, or a town, or a major city, or even an entire nation, but only now is it possible for us to destroy our whole world so fast that nothing can stop it once the process has begun.

That is what makes this point in our history different from any other. And that is what makes this call for each of us to have our own conversation with God so appropriate and so important.

If we want the beauty of the world that we have co-created to be experienced by our children and our children's children, we will have to become spiritual activists right here, right now, and cause that to happen. We must choose to be at cause in the matter.

So, talk with God today. Ask God for help, for counsel and advice, for insight and for strength and for inner peace and for deep wisdom. Ask God on this day to show us how to show up in the world in a way that will cause the world itself to change.

That is the challenge that is placed before every thinking person today.

Now the human soul asks the question: What can I do to preserve the beauty and the wonder of our world and to eliminate the anger and hatred—and the disparity that inevitably causes it— in that part of the world which I touch?

---

*Now the human soul asks the question:
What can I do to preserve the beauty and the
wonder of our world and to eliminate the anger
and hatred—and the disparity that inevitably
causes it— in that part of the world which I touch?*

Please seek to answer that question
today,with all the magnificence that is You.

Neale Donald Walsch

Complacency

I haven't gotten enough sleep in the last few nights, like so many Americans I haven't been able to lure myself away from TV.

Thoughts of various forms of terrorism kept bombarding my mind; disturbing whatever efforts I made to establish some inner peace for myself in the midst of all this madness.

By this morning, my prayers for peace were answered, as I saw some things I hadn't seen before.

We all know that America's heart has been broken this week. But I am reminded of a Carly Simon lyric: "There's more room in a broken heart."

Millions of us are hugging our kids a little tighter, treating our friends and loved ones more tenderly, and counting our blessings for real this week.

Millions of us are hugging our kids a little tighter, treating our friends and loved ones more tenderly, and counting our blessings for real this week.

Also, I don't think that any woman ever again will walk up Madison Avenue in New York City and think that a Gucci bag is all THAT important.

In short, we have been shocked out of a collective stupor this week, and there is benefit in that for all of us.

God can bring good out of anything, even evil. There is nothing that cannot be used to take us closer to the love in our hearts.

For in a state of full despair, of streaming tears and painful sorrow, we become the soft and pliable beings that in fact we truly are.

As it is said in Alcoholics Anonymous, 'Every problem comes bearing its own solution.'

If we allow this crisis to transform us personally, then our country will achieve a badly needed shift in our collective ground of being: spiritual issues will take primacy over material things, love will take primacy over money, and hope and faith will take primacy over cynicism and apathy.

If we allow this crisis to transform us personally, then our country will achieve a badly needed shift in our collective ground of being: spiritual issues will take primacy over material things, love will take primacy over money, and hope and faith will take primacy over cynicism and apathy.

We had become a complacent nation, registering deeply neither the blessings nor the dangers which surrounded us. And now we are complacent no longer.

We have awoken, among other things, to how precious this country is to us, and this week it is not un-hip to say so.

Democracy had become to us just one more

thing that we took for granted, even as we watched it slide further and further away from a living breathing system into an abstract concept more hypocritically revered than vitally practiced.

Well now, Mr. and Mrs. Terrorists— whoever you are and wherever you are— we have remembered what this amazing thing is that we have inherited from our ancestors, and have every intention of bequeathing to our children.

Yes, you were powerful, in a way, for a minute— but only because you caught us sleeping. You woke us up. And you are powerful no more.

Yes, you were powerful, in a way, for a minute— but only because you caught us sleeping. You woke us up. And you are powerful no more.

Whatever it is, Mr. and Ms. Terrorist, that you think you can destroy— our buildings, our communications systems, and our monetary system, even our bodies— what we truly are, you cannot destroy.

For what truly defines us are the ideals at the core of this wounded nation. Buildings can fall and bodies can perish— but those ideals are alive as long as they are alive in any of us.

For what truly defines us are the ideals at the core of this wounded nation.

They are alive in many of us now more powerfully than they had been in years: yes, this is a nation, for all our problems and hypocrisies and mistakes, which has good reason to be on this earth. Which has a destiny yet to fulfill, and gifts still yet to contribute to this world. It has been a blessing on our parents before us, and promises to be a blessing on our children and theirs. We love that idea. We embrace that idea.

No bombs, no terrorism, can kill it or diminish it. It lives in us. And it will live on.

No bombs, no terrorism, can kill it or diminish it. It lives in us. And it will live on.

Amen.

Marianne Williamson

Peace cannot be kept by force. It can only be achieved by understanding.

Albert Einstein

Peace

Amaithi

Nimuhore

Damai

Heiwa

Taika

Sith

Irini

Shantih

Mir

Epilogue

As a chaplain I am trained to see the "highest good" even when things on the outside seem contrary. Yet when the events of September 11, 2001 happened, it was a struggle to see beyond the pain, and to see the "love" or the "good."

The only way I could do this at first was to go into meditation or prayer and be still. When I did this, the words "peace" and "love" kept coming to mind despite all the pain and hurt I felt on the inside.

Then I thought about the Dalai Llama and how his people feel this kind of pain on a daily basis. Then I thought about the great people of the past like Gandhi and Martin Luther King and how they too, witnessed such violence, hatred and attack on a daily basis.

The key to my response to dealing with this tragedy was by following their example. All of them responded to hatred and vengeance with love and peace.

Also, as a person who is constantly seeking great mentors, I wondered what some of the great minds I had studied, like Neale Donald Walsch, Marianne Williamson and others would say about the recent tragedy. What would their perspective be, and what words of wisdom would they say to help me and others move beyond the paralysis of pain to the comfort of healing? Thus this book came to fruition.

All the stories and perspectives you have read, have a common theme. The common theme is love and peace. It is that whatever we do, we must respond with love. And that anger and retaliation only bring about more anger and retaliation.

Also, in order to heal from this event, we must learn from it. We must look at the root cause, and take action to create a more peaceful and loving world.

Thus, I have compiled a list of resources at the end of this book. I know that it will continue to grow, and I know that there are many worthy organizations, media outlets and other groups that I failed to list.

While this book does not offer concrete suggestions or possible solutions, it does offer words of hope, peace and love. With those three tools as our foundation, we will be able to create and discuss positive solutions.

I hope these words of peace and love have comforted you as much as they have me.

I would like to leave you with a story that wraps up all the spiritual principles mentioned in the previous perspectives.

It was Christmas-time at a crowded bus station. One man stood out in the crowd. Why? Because he was obnoxious and rude. He had an angry face filled with hatred; you could see it in his eyes. His forehead was crinkled and he glared at anyone he made eye contact with.

The man reeked of body odor, and his physical appearance was disheveled. He wore mangled clothes, and his facial hair was matted together.

His language was obscene, and under his breath he was cussing at everyone.

Not only that, but he was obscenely drunk. He teetered and stammered as he bumped into anyone in his path. He had no concern for the space of others.

People at the bus station were getting upset at the actions of this vile man. Many of them decided to push him back when he bumped into them.

One young man, pushed the drunken man when he bumped into him, and said, "watch where you're going, Jerk."

As the man pushed the drunken man, he became easily off balance and bumped into more people. Everyone started pushing back and yelling things like, "jerk, scum, etc."

This only fueled the anger already in the man's heart. He cussed louder and became more obscene. Everyone in the bus station was full of anger and disgust.

Suddenly one man pushed the drunken man so hard, that he fell over and landed near a woman sitting on a bench with her eight-year-old daughter.

The eight-year-old girl looked at the man trying to get up, and then looked at her mom. "We should help him, don't you think?" she asked her mom.

The mother responded, "normally, dear, we'd help, but not in this situation. This is different." The mother silently prayed that the vile man would not come over and disturb them.

Suddenly, the little girl got up and went over to the man, who had at this time stood up.

The little girl looked the man directly in the eyes and said, "Sir, why are you so angry?"

The drunken man slurred and yelled at the

little girl to go away. "Leave me alone," he yelled.

The little girl was persistent. She pulled on his shirt and got the man's attention.

"Leave me alone, get away from me," he slurred.

The little girl again, looked him in the eyes and said, "The reason I asked is because I was wondering if there was anything I could do to help?"

The man froze in his tracks. The angry look on his face softened, and he broke into tears.

The three of them; the drunken man, the little girl and the mother, cried together.

They found out that a year ago, the drunken man's wife had died. They had been living paycheck to paycheck as it was and with the high cost of funeral expenses, and the downgrade to only one salary, the man took a turn for the worse. He lost his car and lost his home, and most importantly, he lost the love of his life. He became homeless.

On that day, the year anniversary of his wife's death, he had sold his only winter jacket in order to get bus fare so he could visit his wife at the cemetery.

Many of you may wonder how that story relates to the recent terrorist events. Yet, there are three principles demonstrated in that story that parallel our recent tragedy.

The first is that behind every act of lashing out in anger, there is a deep-rooted pain. We may not know what it is, but the outward manifestation is anger. All anger, has pain at its root.

In order to solve the problem, like Neale Donald Walsch said, we must look at the cause, or the root of the problem.

If we ignore the deep-rooted pain, or the cause of the anger, the cause will not go away and we will never fully heal.

I love Jean Houston's analogy of the recent terrorist events likened to a cancer. To further the analogy, if we rely on the doctors to remove the problem, (like we're relying on government to solve the problem) through surgery, but we continue to smoke, for example, than we haven't solved the root problem, which is the cigarettes. The doctors can keep performing surgery to remove pieces of the diseased lung, but until the culprit (cigarettes) is stopped the problem will continue to manifest.

Second, anger begets anger. In the above story, the angry man angered others. When they retaliated with anger it only fueled the anger that was already in his heart. Eventually, the anger spread throughout the whole bus station, leaving everyone angry. Yet the problem still continued, and was even compounded.

I heard that in Native American tradition they have a saying that says the man who seeks revenge must dig two graves, one for the person he is seeking revenge upon, and one for himself.

This illustrates the principal that anger only begets more anger.

The last principal illustrated in the above example, was that the only thing that could dissolve the man's anger was the pure, innocent love of a child who cared enough to find out what was going on inside the man.

Like Alan Cohen reiterated in his story, the quote from Gandhi that said, "the pure love of one person can offset the hatred of thousands." What a powerful illustration of the power of love.

Keep love in your heart. Spread the word of love and healing to others. If this book has touched you in any way, take the postcard and give it or send it to a friend, family member or coworker. You may request more postcards from our website www.peacefulearth.org. Tell people to order the book on the website or at their local bookstore or at amazon.com.

Read other materials from the contributors of this book. Go to their websites, and contribute to their organizations. Contact and contribute to the groups listed under "Resources." Vote for your favorite peace group on our website.

But most of all, pray for peace. See peace everywhere. Become the Faith Keeper that Alan Cohen talked about. Together, we can all become FaithKeepers in PEACE.

We must heal from this tragedy, but we must not forget it. Like Neale Donald Walsch pointed out, if we forget the lessons, if we don't learn from them and work to re-create a more peaceful and more loving world, than we will never be free from future acts of violence.

Father Leo Booth Biography

"Find the 'You' in Spirit'U'al!" Challenges
Father Leo Booth.

His work as both a priest and a certified
addiction and eating disorder counselor focuses
on the sources and symptoms of wounded spirituality. He challenges the traditional "body-mind-spirit"
model of spirituality, insisting that we cannot create
spiritual wholeness using a model, which puts spirituality in a separate compartment and leaves out the
emotions.

He has created a new spiritual model for
the treatment of depression, addictions and low self-
esteem that teaches how to strengthen the spiritual
connection between body, mind, and emotions so
that people are better able to connect and relate
to the world around them. His books, videos, and
audiocassettes have become part of the curriculum
for treatment centers and therapists.

He knows from personal experience what it is
like to live with no self-esteem. Born in England, he
was educated at King's College in London, England.
Driven and ambitious, he became one of the young-
est rectors in England. He also became an alcoholic.
After a drunk-driving accident in 1977, he entered
treatment for his alcoholism, and has since been
dedicated to working with people suffering from any
addiction or compulsive behavior. As he worked
with recovering addicts of all kinds, he recognized
that negative, unhealthy religious messages play a
major part in creating ingrained guilt and shame.

Thus, Father Leo has created a new spiritual

model for treatment of depressions, addictions and low self-esteem that teaches how to strengthen our spirituality. In 2001, Father Leo celebrates 24 years of sobriety.

Father Leo has appeared on such national television shows as *Oprah, Sally Jessy Raphael, Geraldo,* and others. He is the Program Consultant for Bellwood Health Services in Toronto, Canada, Spiritual Consultant to CADAS in Chattanooga, Tennessee and the author of several books.

Father Leo lectures and workshops at an average of over 100 conferences and seminars annually, worldwide, on topics dealing with all aspects of addiction and spiritual recovery.

Father Leo has over ten publications to his credit to date.

For more information contact:

www.fatherleo.com

Alan Cohen Biography

Alan Cohen, M.A., is the author of twenty popular inspirational books and tapes, including the best-selling *The Dragon Doesn't Live Here Anymore* and the award winning *A Deep Breath of Life.*

He is a contributing writer for the New York Times best-selling series *Chicken Soup for the Soul.* Alan's syndicated column, *From the Heart,* appears in new thought magazines internationally.

Alan brings a warm blend of wisdom, intimacy, humor, and vision to the spiritual path. He loves to extract spiritual lessons from the practical experiences of daily living, and find beauty in the seeming mundane.

Many readers and seminar participants have reported that his teachings have brought them deep comfort, encouragement, and empowerment as they moved through a difficult or transitional phase of their life.

The Celestine Prophecy author, James Redfield describes Alan as "the most eloquent spokesman of the heart," and Dr. Wayne Dyer declares, "Alan Cohen is a major, major player in the spiritual transformation taking place on the planet today. "I love his work and want people to read and APPLY his message."

Alan lives in Maui, Hawaii, where he conducts retreats in spiritual growth and visionary living.

For more information contact:

www.alancohen.com

Terry Cole-Whittaker Biography

Terry Cole-Whittaker is a globally acclaimed inspirational leader and speaker, and world renowned author of best selling books, including *What You Think of Me is None of My Business*, and her newest and most important book, *Every Saint Has A Past, Every Sinner A Future.*

Terry Cole-Whittaker has remained the single most influential trailblazer of her time. The list of her students reads like a who's who of world leaders in every field of endeavor. She was the executive producer and minister of an Emmy Winning six-year international television ministry that reached millions.

10 Women of Power, a best selling book by Laurel King lists Dr. Cole-Whittaker as one of the 10 most powerful and inspirational women in the world. The San Diego Press Club honored her as Woman of the Year, and two times as Headliner of the Year.

She was the recipient of three honorary Doctorate degrees for her humanitarian work and contributions to society. She has been interviewed and featured for her work in the most important magazines, newspapers, television and radio programs in the world.

Under her leadership, as the Founder and Chairman of a non-profit educational foundation, Adventures in Enlightenment, Dr. Cole-Whittaker is building The International Institute of Sacred Knowledge in India, near New Delhi. The work of

"The Institute" is the building of a cultural bridge between the East and the West. Spiritual students from the West will be able to stay at the school and study Vedic culture and will be privileged to receive the teachings of some of the most scholarly and qualified spiritual teachers in the world.

At the present time Dr. Terry and members of her staff are documenting, on audio and videotape, the life and teachings of saintly and scholarly masters of the East as part of the school's Global Library of Sacred Knowledge.

For more information contact:

www.terrycolewhittaker.com

Mark Victor Hansen Biography

Mark Victor Hansen is the New York Times best-selling co-author of the Chicken Soup for the Soul® Series which has currently sold over eighty million copies.

For over 26 years, Mark Victor Hansen has focused solely on helping people in all walks of life reshape their personal vision of what's possible for themselves. From Bangladesh to Birmingham, Mark's keynote messages of possibility, opportunity and action has helped create startling and powerful change in more than 2 million people in 38 countries.

His energy and exuberance travels still further through mediums such as television (Oprah, CNN, Eye to Eye and The Today Show) and print (Time, US News and World Report, USA Today, The New York Times, Entrepreneur Magazine) as he assures our planet's people that "you can easily create the life you deserve."

Mark Victor Hansen has been called one of the "Top 10 Greatest Motivational Speakers." Powerful, life-shifting speakers such as Og Mandino, Zig Ziglar and Jim Rohn count Mark Victor Hansen as one of the most "dynamic and meaningful speakers" of this age. He's even been inducted into the highly acclaimed circle of Horatio Alger recipients because of the remarkable path of life he's created for himself.

Mark Victor Hansen is also a huge philanthropist, with proceeds from all the Chicken Soup for the Soul® Series going to various charities. Mark Victor Hansen himself is committed to tithing both his money and his ideas.

For more information contact:

www.markvictorhansen.com

www.chickensoup.com

Jean Houston Biography

Dr. Jean Houston is a scholar and researcher in human capacities, and for the past 30 years has co-directed, with her husband Dr. Robert Masters, the Foundation for Mind Research. Their work has focused on the understanding of latent human abilities. She is the founder of the Mystery School—a program of cross-cultural mythic and spiritual studies—dedicated to teaching history, philosophy, the new physics, psychology, anthropology, myth, and the many dimensions of our human potential.

Dr. Houston was the protégé of the late anthropologist Margaret Mead, who instructed her in the workings of organizations and power structures in many different cultures. With the late mythologist Joseph Campbell, Jean Houston frequently co-led seminars and workshops aimed at understanding interrelationships between ancient myths and modern societies.

Additionally, Jean Houston has made cross-cultural studies of educational and healing methods in Asia and Africa. Dr. Houston's mind has been called "a national treasure".

As Advisor to UNICEF in human and cultural development, she has worked to implement some of their extensive educational and health programs, primarily in Myanmar [Burma] and Bangladesh.

A past President of the Association for Humanistic Psychology [1977], she has taught philosophy, psychology, and religion at the university level.

Since 1959, she has spoken at hundreds of colleges and universities. She has directed two three-year courses in human capacities development and a program of cross-cultural mythic and spiritual studies, now in its thirteenth year.

In 1984, she devised a national not-for-profit organization, called The Possible Society, to encourage the creation of new ways for people to work together to help solve societal problems.

In 1985, Dr. Houston was awarded the Distinguished Leadership Award from the Association of Teacher Educators. In 1993, she received the Gardner Murphy Humanitarian Award and the INTA Humanitarian of the Year award. In 1994, she received the Lifetime Outstanding Creative Achievement Award from the Creative Education Foundation.

Among her books are *Public Like a Frog, The Hero and The Goddess, The Possible Human, The Search for the Beloved, Godseed, Life Force, Listening to the Body, Manual for the Peacemaker, The Passion of Isis and Osiris*. Harper/San Francisco published her autobiography, *A Mythic Life: Learning to Live Our Greater Stories.*

For more information contact:

www.jeanhouston.org

Dan Millman Biography

Dan Millman is a former world trampoline champion, Stanford gymnastics coach, and Oberlin College professor.

His books, including *Way of the Peaceful Warrior, Sacred Journey, The Life You Were Born to Live, Everyday Enlightenment, The Laws of Spirit,* and more recently, *Living on Purpose* have inspired millions of readers in more than twenty languages.

Also an international lecturer and seminar leader, Dan continues to influence people from all walks of life, including leaders in the fields of health, psychology, education, business, politics, entertainment, sports, and the arts.

Dan and his family live in northern California.

Mahatma Gandhi said, "My life is my teaching." What I write is only as true and useful as what I live.

For more information contact:

www.danmillman.com

Mary Manin Morrissey Biography

Mary serves as the founder and spiritual leader of Living Enrichment Center. The Center, headquartered in Wilsonville, Oregon, on 95-forested acres, is one of the fastest growing churches in America and has been described as the 21st Century Church in the making.

Today the Reverend Mary Manin Morrissey is the senior minister of the Living Enrichment Center serving more than 3,000 people weekly, with radio outreach to more than 80 countries.

Mary could have let her life be limited by circumstance and feelings of unworthiness. She was tested by life-threatening illness and by years of struggling to make ends meet as she raised four children. Through it all, she clung to her determination to become an ordained minister and a counselor.

Today, her message transforms the lives of countless individuals.

Mary Manin Morrissey is also the author of two books: *Building Your Field of Dreams* and more recently, *No Less Than Greatness* by Bantam.

For more information contact:

www.lecworld.org

Dr. Angelo Pizelo Biography

Dr. Angelo Pizelo is a professional educator and an ordained minister of religious science. He holds academic degrees (B.A., M.A., and PhD) in school administration and has a Doctor of Divinity degree.

He has forty years of experience as a teacher, administrator and superintendent of schools and was a Superintendent Emeritus of the Bass Lake Joint Union School District.

He is the Founder of the Educational Enhancement Foundation, the Positive Living Center of Central California, Inc. and the Emerson Theological Institute.
He is also the Founder of Project Spice (Seniors Participating In Community Education.)

He is currently the President of Emerson Institute and Director of the Positive Living Center of Central California, Inc. and Educational Consultant to the Bass Lake Joint Union School District.

He serves as a director on the Affiliated New Thought Network, Board of Directors.

He has received numerous awards including: The California School Leadership Award, The Five Counties Labor Council's Community Services Award, The Rotary Club's Business Person of the Year Award, The Lions Club Outstanding Achievement Award and numerous other awards including the Oakhurst Citizen of the Year Award.

Dr. Pizelo was also listed in the Who's Who "Among Outstanding Business Executives."

Dr. Pizelo is married to Dr. Stella Pizelo and

has two children, Anna and Nicole.

He currently resides in Oakhurst California, only 14 miles from the southern gates of Yosemite National Park.

For more information contact:

www.emersoninstitute.edu

Bob Proctor Biography

For 40 years, Bob Proctor has focused his entire agenda around helping people create lush lives of prosperity, rewarding relationships and spiritual awareness.

Bob Proctor knows how to help *you* because he comes from a life of want and limitation himself. In 1960, he was a high-school dropout with a resume of dead-end jobs and a future clouded in debt.

One book was placed in his hands— *Napoleon Hill's Think and Grow Rich*— that planted the seed of hope in Bob's mind. In just months, and with further support from the works of Earl Nightingale, Bob's life literally spun on a dime. In a year, he was making more than $100,000, and soon topped the $1 million mark.

Bob then moved to Chicago to work for his real-life mentors, Earl Nightingale and Lloyd Conant. After rising to the position of Vice President of Sales at Nightingale-Conant, he established his own seminar company.

Bob Proctor now travels the globe, teaching thousands of people how to believe in and act upon the greatness of their own minds.

Bob Proctor is also the author of *You Were Born Rich.*

For more information contact:

www.bobproctor.com

Neale Donald Walsch Biography

Neale Donald Walsch is a 57-year-old modern day spiritual messenger living in the hills of Ashland, Oregon whose words are touching the world.

He has written 15 books on spirituality and its practical application in every day life, including the multi-millions-selling five-book *With God* series-*Conversations with God*-Books 1, 2, 3, *Friendship with God* and *Communion with God*-each of which has found it way to the New York Times Best Seller List. *Conversations with God*-Book 1 occupied that list for over 130 weeks.

He has dedicated his life to spreading the message of these books, the impact of which has been felt around the globe, with books in the *With God* series having been translated into 27 languages.

Mr. Walsch is the founder of the ReCreation Foundation, a non-profit organization with planetary outreach whose mission it is to give people back to themselves.

The foundation sponsors a prison outreach program, a homeless persons ministry, an undertaking to place the thrust of its spiritual message of the Oneness of All Humans in community-level health centers as part of Whole Wellness programs, an outreach to the world's gay and lesbian community, an outreach to the world's teen population, a New Form Education program called The Heartlight School based on concepts found in the *With God* books, and spiritual growth workshops and retreats around the world.

He is also founder of Greatest Visions, a for-profit company dedicated to spreading the message of the *With God* books utilizing the tools of commerce, and to transforming the way we do business in America and around the world by encouraging the creation of a new reason to do business, and a new definition of the word "profit."

Mr. Walsch is also the creator of Millennium Legacies, Inc., a New Wave communications company that operates Walsch Music and Walsch Books, also to send the message of the *With God* books to larger and larger audiences through artists and authors using other articulations.

Neale Donald Walsch is the co-founder of the New Millennium Peace Foundation, sponsors of The Humanity Conference in Seoul, South Korea in June, 2001, a gathering of leading edge thinkers called together to consider new ways to address the challenge of bringing last peace to the world.

For more information contact:

www.conversationswithgod.com

Marianne Williamson Biography

Marianne Williamson is the author of numerous best-selling books, including *A Return to Love, A Woman's Worth, Illuminata,* and *Healing the Soul of America.*

Ms. Williamson is a popular and prominent lecturer, most noted for her discussions on the teachings of *A Course In Miracles.*

Ms. Williamson is the spiritual leader of the nation's second largest Unity church. She is the cofounder of the Global Renaissance Alliance and the guiding force behind her most recent book, *Imagine: What America Could Be in the 21st Century.*

For more information contact:

www.marianne.com

About the Editor

Lisa Hepner has studied spiritual growth for over ten years. After leaving a lucrative career in the medical field, she decided to pursue her dream of writing and also start her own business developing an inspirational product line.

She is an entrepreneur, starting a business called *Hold the Vision*, which creates inspirational products.

She is a chaplain at the Living Enrichment Center in Wilsonville, Oregon. She is taking course-work to become a New Thought Practitioner.

She believes in tithing and also believes in donating money to various causes and organizations. All of her projects benefit some organization or group.

For more information contact:

www.lisahepner.com

*If you love peace, then hate injustice, hate tyranny,
hate greed— but hate these things in yourself,
not in another.*

Mahatma Gandhi

Peace

Vrede

Salaam

He Ping

Mir

Paix

Hetep

Frieden

Sipala

Resources

Please make sure to read the biographies of all those who contributed stories, and check out their websites, organizations or reading materials.

Here are some other organizations or even individuals that have started campaigns, that you may be interested in contacting or finding out more information about. Please feel free to suggest other organizations or groups for future editions of this book.

911 Peace Organization
www.9-11peace.org
See article, "Why Peace?"

Amnesty International
www.aiusa.org
322 Eighth Avenue
New York, NY 10001
(212) 807-8400

Association for Global New Thought
www.agnt.org
1514 Main St. #2
Evanston, IL 60202
(847) 866-9525

Center for the Advancement of non violence
www.nonviolenceworks.com
1223 Wilshire Blvd. #472
Santa Monica, CA 90403

Coalition for World Peace
www.actionla.org/peaceAction group containing
events and flyers

Common Dreams
www.commondreams.org
P.O. Box 443
Portland, ME 04112
(207) 799-2185

Fellowship of Reconciliation
www.forusa.org
P.O. Box 271
Nyack, NY 10960
(845) 358-4601

Fritjof Capra, Ph.D.
www.fritjofcapra.net
Center for Ecoliteracy
Excellent paper on web that explains cause of terrorism along with solutions.

The Foundation for a Healing Among Nations
15237 Sunset Blvd. #111
Palisades, CA 90272
(310) 230-9774

M.K. Gandhi Institute for Nonviolence
www.gandhiinstitute.org
Christian Brothers University
650 East Parkway South
Memphis, TN 38104
(901) 452-2824

Genesis: Foundation for the Universal Human
www.universalhuman.org
P.O. Box 339
Ashland, OR 97520
1-888-440-7685

Global Exchange
www.globalexchange.org
2017 Mission Street #303
San Francisco, CA 94110
(415) 255-7296

Global Renaissance Alliance
www.renaissancealliance.org
P.O. Box 3259
Centerline, MI 48015
(541) 890-4716

Gylian Creed
gyliancreed@youremergentself.net
Organizes monthly peace movement.

Institute for Global Communication
www.igc.org
P.O. Box 29904
San Francisco, CA 94129-0904
(415) 561-6100,

Institute of Noetic Sciences
www.noetic.org
101 San Antonio Road
Petaluma, CA 94952
(707) 775-3500

Interfaith Voices for Peace and Justice
www.interfaithvoices.org
P.O. Box 270214
St. Louis, MO 63127
(888) 454-8296

Let's Keep America Going
www.letskeepamericagoing.com
CD on how to beat terrorism by Mark Victor Hansen
and Debra Jones.

Mercy Corp
www.mercyvolunteers.org
1325 Sumneytown Pike
Gwynedd Valley, PA 19437
(215) 641-5535

New Dimensions World Broadcasting Network
P.O. Box 569
Ukiah, CA 95482
(707) 468-5215

Peace Corps
www.peacecorps.gov
The Paul D. Coverdell Peace Corps headquarters
111 20th Street NW
Washington, D.C. 20526
1-800-424-8580

Positive Futures Network
www.futurenet.org
P.O. Box 10818
Bainbridge Island, WA 98110-0818
(206)842-0216

Posters for Peace
www.postersforpeace.org
A wide selection of peace posters.

ReCreation Foundation
www.conversationswithgod.org
PMB #1150
1257 Siskiyou Blvd.
Ashland, OR 97520
(541) 482-8806

Rose Rose-Tree
www.Rose-Rosetree.com.
Book reviewer and author, *Empathic Volunteer Work.*

Seattle Coalition
www.scn.org
Multiple peace references

Spirituality & Health
www.spiritualityhealth.com
Has wonderful peace quotes from many famous
people. Compiled by Frederic and May Ann Brussat.

UNICEF
www.unicef.org
3 United Nations Plaza
New York, NY 10017
(212) 887-7465

Washington Peace Center
www.washingtonpeacecenter.org
1801 Columbia Rd. NW Ste 104
Washington, DC 2009
(202)234-2000

Wisdom
www.wisdommedia.com
P.O. Box 1546
Bluefield, WV 24701
1-888-894-7638

World Peace Meditation

Join in the **World Peace Meditation** at noon Greenwich time on **December 31st** of every year.

The mission of World Healing Day on December 31st is to declare "a planetary affirmation of peace and love, and forgiveness and understanding which involves millions of people in a simultaneous global mind link."

The movement began in 1986, with an idea from John Randolph Price. Noon Greenwich time was selected as the time because it would encompass all time zones during that twenty-four hour time period.

On December 31st 1986, more than five hundred million people from all walks of life and religious backgrounds all over the country said a prayer for peace at the same time.

For more information see:
http://lonestar.texas.net/~quartus

Times:

Pacific Standard Time 4:00 A.M.
Mountain Standard Time 5:00 A.M.
Central Standard Time 6:00 A.M.
Eastern Standard Time 7:00 A.M.

Acknowledgments

First and foremost, I would like to acknowledge the presence of God in my life and flowing through my life, and serving as my Divine Source and Supply.

I want to express my gratitude and my love for my Soul Partner on this Earth, Christopher Farmer. Chris, I wouldn't have been able to do all this without your support. It's an invaluable gift you have given me; the gift of your time, your support, your commitment and your love. I would also like to thank Paul Farmer for help in editing the final manuscript.

I would like to thank all the authors, who took time out of their busy schedules to submit their stories and allow their voices to be heard. The world is a better place because of their existence.

My love and gratitude to my family: Paul and Anna Hepner, Jay and Jane Tidmore (mom) and my brother, Paul Hepner. Mom and Paul, thanks for helping me when I needed it most. I could never repay you for all the wonderful things you've done and the support you've given. This book would not have been possible without your support.

Thanks to my extended family: Shannon Walker and Galen and Paula Walker. My love goes to my two animal children, Tigger and Talmage.

I would like to thank all my friends on my spiritual journey. Linda Mueller, my Mastermind partner and dearest friend. Linda, thanks for believing in me and seeing the best in me when I couldn't see it. I would not be where I am today without your prayers, confidence and love. You are my angel.

Jennifer Omner, thank you for your loving support also.

I would like to acknowledge those who have given me spiritual support and advice, Ted Brunell and Byron and Mari Haley. You are all very wise and I have learned so much from you.

I am grateful for my spiritual home, the Living Enrichment Center, and the growth that it has supported. Thanks to my fellow chaplains who nourish my soul. Thanks to Sally Rutis for all her wonderful work and help.

I am thankful to my many mentors: Bill O'Hearn, you are an inspiration, and a role model. You have always believed in me, from the moment I met you, and you have one of the biggest hearts I've ever seen. Bob Ross, you taught me to see the strength in myself and to follow my dreams.

Thanks to Fred Dickey and Jerri Wilson for being so supportive, and to Dave and Joyce Hayes for always being there.

And, thanks to all my friends in Toastmasters. You all have allowed me to grow and conquer my fears and have fun in the process.

I give thanks for all the people who have touched my life in the past, and for all those I have yet to meet who will grace my life in the future.

God Bless You.

Order Information

To order more copies of this book send check or money order for $12.00 plus $4.00 S&H to the address below.

Peaceful Earth
c/o Hold the Vision
14845 SW Murray Scholls Dr.
Ste 110, PMB #302
Beaverton, OR 97007

Phone (503) 524-7151
Fax (503) 590-6218

Or you may order online at:
www.peacefulearth.org

Note: Proceeds from the purchase of this book benefit organizations promoting spiritual growth and world peace.

If you would like to receive more postcards to hand out to friends and family, please contact us.

Order Information

To order more copies of this book send check or money order for $12.00 plus $4.00 S&H to the address below.

Peaceful Earth
c/o Hold the Vision
14845 SW Murray Scholls Dr.
Ste 110, PMB #302
Beaverton, OR 97007

Phone (503) 524-7151
Fax (503) 590-6218

Or you may order online at:
www.peacefulearth.org

Note: Proceeds from the purchase of this book benefit organizations promoting spiritual growth and world peace.

If you would like to receive more postcards to hand out to friends and family, please contact us.